C000241564

The Special Gift of Women

for God, the Family & the World

by
Dr Maria Fedoryka
Professor of Philosophy
Ave Maria University

*All booklets are published thanks to the
generous support of the members of the
Catholic Truth Society*

CATHOLIC TRUTH SOCIETY
PUBLISHERS TO THE HOLY SEE

Contents

Introduction

The human person is a being of extraordinary dignity. All of creation reflects God, revealing in some small way His majesty, His goodness, His beauty. But the human person is not only a reflection of God, revealing Him in distant and weak way, but has been created in His very "image and likeness". This means that man glorifies God incomparably more than any other of His creatures. How so? All other creatures glorify God simply through the gifts that God has given them; all that they have, comes directly from Him. But in the case of the human person, something extraordinary takes place: the human person has the privilege of *himself* contributing to God's glory – with his understanding and especially with his freedom.

The glory that God receives when man becomes *good* far exceeds the glory He receives from the brightness of sun, or the loveliness of the flower, or the majesty of the mountains. Nothing in creation is more beautiful than a person shining with *virtue* – that dazzling jewel that comes to be only in the soul that has *cooperated freely* with God's gifts.

With this in mind, we turn to considering "the gift of woman" – a phrase which for us takes on a double meaning: we will consider what it is that the woman has received from God as a gift entrusted to her, which she then returns to Him, developing and bringing it to perfection – for God's glory, for the good of those whose lives she touches, and for her own happiness.

We find the following striking passage addressed to women in the Second Vatican Council's closing speech:

> As you know, the Church is proud to have glorified and liberated woman, and in the course of the centuries, in diversity of characters, to have brought into relief her basic equality with man. But the hour is coming, in fact has come, when the vocation of woman is being achieved in its fullness, the hour in which woman acquires in the world an influence, an effect and a power never hitherto achieved. That is why, at this moment when the human race is undergoing so deep a transformation, women impregnated with the spirit of the Gospel can do so much to aid mankind in not falling.[1]

These stirring words cannot fail to touch in the depth of her being the woman who reads them. We find here expressed on the one hand the great dignity of the woman: she is a creature whom "God has willed for its own sake", in the words of *Gaudium et spes*.[2] This means that her dignity is so great, that it does not come from being useful for some purpose beyond herself. Her dignity is found in her *simply because of who she is* – a creature who reflects God in her own completely irreplaceable way. This means that she may never be used as an instrument by others, who would use her for their own ends, taking away her freedom. She has the privilege and the duty to direct herself *freely* to her destiny.

But this passage is also saying something else, something that shows us how mysterious and paradoxical the human person is: it is telling us that the woman will become fulfilled *only if she makes a gift of herself to others*. Above we saw *Gaudium et spes* telling us that "man is the only creature on earth that God has willed for its own sake". But it then immediately adds, "and man cannot fully find himself *except through a sincere gift of himself*."[3] We hear echoed here Christ's words, that "unless a seed fall to the ground and dies, it will not bear fruit". What is true in the world of nature is even more true in the world of persons: it is only when we live for others, in a sense "forgetting" ourselves – it is only then that we become fulfilled. It is only then that we shine with virtues, which are the truest adornment of the human soul.

The encyclical *Mulieris dignitatem* – translated as "The Dignity of Woman" – discovers every woman's vocation by looking to the greatest woman, the Blessed Virgin Mary. John Paul II writes: "the special presence of the Mother of God in the mystery of the Church makes us

6

think of the exceptional link between this 'woman' and the whole human family."[4] Mary plays a central role in her service to the Church, which forms all of humanity for its destiny in God. Reflecting Mary's role, all woman are called to give themselves to others, playing a crucial role in the formation of humanity.

Male and female:
two ways of being, two vocations

Male and female

All persons are made in the image and likeness of God, but we find, mysteriously, that humanity is divided into two kinds of persons: man and woman. Let us think about this for a moment. We could say that every person is "three dimensional", with 1) the dimension of human nature, 2) the dimension of being male or female, and 3) the dimension of individuality. On the deepest level, all persons are identical, simply in having a human nature. On the third level, in their individuality, each person is entirely unique, wholly different from every other person, and therefore completely irreplaceable. But we could say that between these two dimensions, there exists a third one, a dimension in which humanity is divided into two "modes": every human person exists as *masculine* or as *feminine*, as a man or as a woman. These are often referred to as the two genders. While men and women have in common all the features of human nature, masculinity and femininity permeate their entire being, "coloring" the soul, the psyche, and the body of each.

Some contemporary trends would have us believe that masculinity and femininity are nothing but a social invention, something that we acquire simply through the pressure of customs that happen to be adopted by a community. It is true that our environment plays some role in who we become as men and as women in certain aspects of our life; and one cannot accept a notion of masculinity and femininity which is so narrow and fixed as to deny of men and women abilities or characteristics that are proper to every person as person. But the deepest and most important characteristics of masculinity and femininity are clearly not fabricated by our conventions, and exist in human persons prior to the influences of society. Those who would deny this have the difficult task of going against the evidence of all ages and all cultures, not to mention our own experience. The differences between man and woman manifest themselves too early to be socially conditioned, and form too fundamental a part of our being to have been created merely by social convention.

In fact, however, masculinity and femininity are first and foremost spiritual characteristics, that reflect something of God's being, something very significant. St. John tells us of the great mystery hidden from the ages, revealed in Christ: that God is Love. He is a trinity of persons, made up of an eternal movement of complete and perfect self-giving and receiving (the Father and the Son) from which springs another person as its fruit (the Holy Spirit). By a marvelous invention, these two gestures of love are translated into two ways of being a human person, in God's creation of humanity as man and woman.

While our fallen human condition makes it often seem that man and woman are pitted against each other, we see that the original and true meaning of this division is that a unique love union should be possible between them in marriage. Rather than being *opposites*, as certain feminists might have it, the difference between them should be characterized as *complementary*. We could call it a "friendly difference", like two notes that are different yet harmonious, each one as it were showing the other to its best advantage.

Besides the union in marriage which the difference between them makes possible, it is the case that man and woman give joy to each other, simply in being different in this complementary way. The world is more wonderful place for men because of the presence of women in it, and a more wonderful place for women because of the presence of men.

The difference between men and women has another side to it: each is an *enrichment* for the other. The gifts of men and women are different – and these gifts enrich not only the one possessing them, but others as well, as man and woman give of themselves in service. The strengths that each one has equips them for different forms of service to those around them – for it is for *service* that their gifts were given to them. This means that men and women, while both are called to live all the virtues, each becomes a witness to the other of the virtues that come from their gifts, and remind the other that he is called to live these virtues as well. It also means that they are each called to different tasks or roles – the tasks that require the special strengths that each has.

Different gifts reveal different vocations

What, then, are these different ways in which men and women serve humanity? To discover them, we look to the deepest service that man and woman can offer to God and to other persons: the service of *fatherhood* and the service of *motherhood*. These, in turn, are inseparably connected to the state of being *husband* and *wife*. Let us look at this more closely.

However it is lived, whether physically in marriage, or spiritually in consecrated virginity, *married love* – the love between husband and wife – is what brings the person to his highest fulfillment. This is because married love is the *total self-gift* of one person to another – and as we saw, self-giving is the vocation of every person.

If we reflect on this, we see that the love between husband and wife comes to its fulfillment when they become *parents*. What happens when the two becomes parents, and why is this a fulfillment of their love? The coming to be of the child is an overflow of the spouses' love for each other. It is as if this love is so deep, and so great, that it cannot contain itself, and wants to share itself with a totally new being, to draw that new being into the love! It is here, when love reaches its end point in the child, that the different roles of man and woman stand before our eyes in a new and clear way. The father and the mother are both to care for the child, but each does so in a way that is proper to their gifts.

And so it is in reflecting on motherhood, the highest expression of femininity, that we discover the special gifts and the vocation of women. This is true, whether the woman is a mother biologically, or only spiritually; motherhood is an attitude of the heart, to which all women are called. We will reflect on motherhood, to discover the qualities unique to the woman, by which she will serve humanity.

The special gift of the woman

How we discover the woman's vocation

We saw that the human person is the only being in nature created in the image and likeness of God. When we encounter a being with such great dignity, what is the response that we should give to this precious being? Is respect enough? Is admiration enough? Esteem? Reverence? John Paul II tells us that none of these is sufficient. There is only one response that does the job – and that response is *love*. "The person must be loved", writes the former pope, "since love alone corresponds to what the person is."[5] Next to love, all other responses are partial and feeble; none can compare with the completeness, the totality, and the depth of love. Love seems to include in itself all of these other attitudes, but goes far beyond them; without love, all of these other responses remain "cold".

In the case of the human being, God so willed it that the person enters the world *totally dependent on another*. No other being in creation is as completely helpless as is the human infant. The one to whom the human person in his infancy is first entrusted, and that in a most radical way, is the *woman*, the mother. We see this first on a physical level: the woman gives the child her own body, her own physical energy, without which the child could not survive. The woman is fashioned by God for this service to another, the structure of her body is "equipped" for this service. But this physical dependence of the child on the woman is a weak reflection of a much more important dependence: *a dependence of the child on the mother not only as a physical being, but as a being with a spiritual soul*.

What is the "nourishment" that the child, as more than a physical being, needs? What is the "food" that enables the child to survive as a person? At this early stage, the child is in need of a *delicate, deeply attentive, unconditional, and every-present love*. This kind of love is an absolute condition for the child to survive and to flourish as a person. Both parents are called to love the child, with a total love. But each has a special role in how they live that love. The special love of the woman as mother has often been called a *"nurturing love"*, while the love of the father is referred to as *"protective love"*. It is the need of the child for being nurtured in this way that calls out the woman's specific gifts when it comes to loving, and shows us her special vocation.

"Receptivity" as the key to the nature of the feminine

This unique ability to love is rooted in the key feature of femininity, *receptivity*. The feminine soul – which is reflected in the woman's psyche and in her body – is fashioned by God as uniquely open and receptive to the what is beyond it, ready to *accept* and *affirm* everything simply as it is. This is contrasted with the masculine soul, which, in reflecting God's self-giving, has been fashioned to take initiative, to "make" and to "do" for the sake of others. Women witness to men the call of every human person to be receptive to others, and especially to God; while men witness to women the call of every human person to be active participators in the world around them, especially in the work of their own salvation.

The special qualities of a mother's love

Receptivity is the special quality that explains why the child has been entrusted to her in the earliest stages of its life, depending on her for the love that it needs. What then are the characteristics of a mother's love?

a. Special sensitivity of the woman to the person simply as person

Firstly, the woman has a unique capacity to receive the person in all their dignity as a person, and as an individual. The woman is able to recognise a person as one who has a value apart from their "usefulness" and even apart from their specific gifts; the woman is able to see the person as one who is infinitely precious simply in being the irreplaceable person that God has made them. The child does not have to "do" or "accomplish" anything to be loved by the mother. The mother's affirmation is offered unconditionally – because her gaze is fixed on the child's deepest center, which always remains valuable beyond measure.

This is what John Paul II means when he writes: "The unique contact with the new human being developing within her gives rise to an attitude towards human beings – not only towards her own child, but every human being – which profoundly marks the woman's personality. It is commonly thought that *women* are more capable than men of paying attention t*o another person*, and that motherhood develops this predisposition even more."[6]

The mother's unconditional welcome of the child lays the basis for what we call "self-esteem" – the person's fundamental sense of their self-worth. A person cannot on their own experience their preciousness; just as we need a mirror to see our own eyes, so only in the loving gaze of another does the child sees "mirrored back" to him his own inherent value.

Everything that happens in the child's early life becomes like a root which anchors him for the rest of his life. When the child that has been truly loved by his mother enters into the ups and downs of adulthood, he will still feel his value in the midst of failures, but also realize that successes are not the measure of his worth. Schooled in this way by his mother's love, the child will also be prepared to treat others in the same way – to always recognize their basic worth as persons, and to affirm them according to this worth.

b. The woman gives herself in a total way

There is a second important characteristic of love typical to the feminine nature. The woman has a special readiness to give of her very *self*, and in a *total way*. The woman does not just give *things* to the child out of love, or just a *part* of herself, her time, her services. Instead, she stands ready *at every moment* to give what the child needs; and when she gives it, she gives *her very self* along with that service.

In this way, the woman is the first to teach the child that love involves the giving of one's very self to the beloved. Faced with this self-giving of the mother, the child learns the other essential aspect of love: receptivity. In love, one must stand ready to receive the other unconditionally, just as one is accepted unconditionally. And we will see in the next point, how the intimacy of the mother's love, its immediate and concrete presence to the child, are so important in learning this dimension of love.

c. Tender closeness: another gift of the mother

This is the final important quality to a mother's love that we will look at: *tender intimacy* or *closeness*. All love requires intimacy; without it, love is not fully love. There are two sides to the intimacy of love: a spiritual side, found in the emotions, and a physical side, found in touch. There is in the woman a unity of body, mind, and heart, that makes it possible for her to live easily and naturally this characteristic of love.

Firstly, the woman has a special capacity for love that is rich with the *warmth of emotion* or *affectivity*.[7] Emotions contribute to the completion of love; without them, love may be known by the *mind*, but it is not *felt*. And without being felt, love does not really hit home. How many people have suffered, because while their mothers may have performed many actions that may point to love – such as cooking for them, seeing to their physical needs, seeing to their education – these mothers did not convey love to their child with the glowing warmth of emotion. Somehow, without emotion, we do not feel that we are being truly "seen" with the eyes of love, and so not being seen as the precious individual that we are.[8]

The second side of the intimacy of love is *physical touch*. At the early stage in a person's life, physical contact is important for conveying the warmth of love. Emotions have a "spiritual radiance" to them, but for the infant, who is still totally immersed in the physical, touch plays a very important role in their experience of love. The child is completely dependent on the mother for all of his physical needs. It is beautiful to recognise that the physical touch involved in this care then becomes for the mother a way of loving the child. Because of the close unity between body and soul in the woman, love flows easily from the mother's heart into her body, spontaneously communicating itself physically to the child which has been given to her. Love has really hit home.

Summary of motherly love

Entrusted with the human person in the most formative stage of his life, the woman has received the gifts that allow her to fulfill this task. John Paul II writes, "The moral and spiritual strength of a woman is joined to her awareness that God entrusts the human being to her in a special way. Of course, God entrusts every human being to each and every other human being. But this entrusting concerns women in a special way – precisely by reason of their femininity – and this in a particular way determines their vocation."[9] Theodore Ratisbonne, in his biography of St. Bernard of Clairvaux, captures in a beautiful way the unique gift of the mother to the child:

> Blessed is the man whose infancy has been watched over, kindled, penetrated by the eye of a tender and holy mother. That glance has a magical power over the soul of the child; it beams forth sweetness and life; and, as the sun's rays mature the fruits of the earth, and sweeten them by the communication of its own substance, so does the mother deposit, in the soul of the child, the sacred character of love. St. Bernard had this inestimable blessing.[10]

The vocation of all women to a "nurturing" love

Just as love is the most important element in a child's life, and is provided for in a unique way by the mother – so love is always and everywhere the most important reality of human existence. Not only the woman who is a mother physically, but every woman has the special gift and calling of keeping the paramount importance of love vibrantly, even if discreetly, present in whatever sphere she finds herself. In doing this she preserves the truth that in all of our earthly endeavors, the human person must remain at the center.[11] Whether in business, or education, or technology, or in any other area, nothing has meaning if it does not safeguard the dignity of the human person, respect his rights, and contribute to his flourishing. But only the reality of love keeps the person at the center of our vision. Love alone stands fully at the service of the person. John Paul II speaks of this particular contribution of woman as her "genius":

> In our own time, the successes of science and technology make it possible to attain material well-being to a degree hitherto unknown. While this favors some, it pushes others to the margins of society. In this way, unilateral progress can also lead to a gradual loss of sensitivity for man, that is, for what is essentially human. In this sense, our time in particular awaits the manifestation of that "genius" which

belongs to women, and which can ensure sensitivity for human beings in every circumstance: because they are human! – And because the greatest of these is love (cf. 1 *Cor* 13:13).[12]

The woman is the one to whom God gave the special gift of being receptive to *persons*, of seeing persons as persons, and not simply as intersecting with their own needs and projects. There is a unity between the woman's heart, mind, and body that allows her to keep a proper order in the relationship between all our undertakings, and the importance of persons. She has been bestowed with the "talent" of warmth and suppleness of heart in order that she may radiate the acceptance and affirmation of unconditional love to those around her.

Compassion – another gift and call of the woman

This vocation to love is inseparable from another specific gift of the woman: a sensitivity for the suffering of others, and a willingness to join in that suffering. In his encyclical on suffering, called *Salvifici dolores*, John Paul II included a major section on the call for *compassion* in the face of suffering. He is clear that *every single person* – whether man or woman – has a solemn obligation to live compassion. But the woman, in virtue of her gifts, can be a special "witness" to this virtue, helping men to develop compassion within themselves. This is one of the ways that the complementarity between male and female becomes fruitful.

Suffering is a great mystery – we could say that in a way it is the greatest puzzle of human life. It has no natural resolution, and is in itself unbearable. But there is a kind of solution to the mystery, insofar something wonderful happens because of suffering. A new intensity of love comes into being, which changes suffering, if not taking it away, surrounding it with its opposite: a deep consolation and even happiness. John Paul II writes, "...we could say that suffering, which is present under so many different forms in our human world, is also present in order *to unleash love in the human person*, that unselfish gift of one's 'I' on behalf of other people, especially those who suffer."[13]

To be compassionate does not simply mean to do something that takes away or makes the suffering easier; in most cases, we are not able to do that. Compassion is a "suffering with" the one who suffers. What a consolation, when someone in the dark loneliness of suffering suddenly finds with him in that dark place a sensitive heart – a heart that is hurting because he is hurting, and suffering with him, out of love! As Mother Teresa said, suffering is unbearable only when one suffers alone.

The woman's vocation to an intimate and deeply personal love goes along with her ability to be in this deeply consoling way with and for the one who suffers.

In her receptivity of the other, in her great sensitivity of heart, the woman is able to be a witness to the need for courage in remaining vulnerable to the pain of another; she is a witness to the call for selflessness in taking on another's wounds.

Woman as spiritual bride and mother

Many women live their gifts within the family; many live it without having their own children, but just by being available to those around them in a womanly way. But there is yet another way for a woman to live her vocation: in a supernatural way, as a consecrated spouse of Christ. This grace of a special call does not do away with the deepest makeup of the woman, but on the contrary, takes it up and perfects it.

There is a great mystery in the call of the woman to become a bride of Christ. To be invited to enter into an exclusive and total self-giving as the *bride* of the omnipotent God, creator of heaven and earth, the one who is Holiness Itself...is a mystery that we will not understand in this life. Needless to say, it is pure gift, something we could never have imagined on our own.

To the extent that we can understand it, we will do so only in the light of *love*. If we understand that this all-powerful God *is Himself* love, and that He therefore not only wishes the salvation of His creatures, but thirsts for a close union with His creatures, we will catch a glimpse of what is at the heart of this mystery: God invites some of His creatures to live in an exclusive relationship of love with Him. Consecrated virginity can, in fact, be summed up as "a state of love"; its very heart is love; without love, the religious state is like a body without a soul.[14] So the state of consecrated becomes another way for the woman to live the vocation to a deep, tender, and intimate love.[15]

It is easy to see that in consecrated virginity, the vocation of the woman to motherhood is actually greatly expanded. The woman's love is now directed to God Himself – and through this, to all of humanity. Just as an earthly husband and wife enters into everything that the other loves and holds dear, so, too, the consecrated virgin enters into God's love of all persons. Love for humanity becomes how the consecrated woman exercises the gift of motherhood: she becomes supernaturally fruitful through the love of Christ. John Paul II writes, "Spousal love – with its maternal potential hidden in the heart of the woman as a virginal bride – when joined to Christ, the Redeemer of each and every person, is also predisposed to being open to each and every person."[16]

Finally, in her femininity, the woman religious plays a unique role in being a "sign" to all lay persons of their ultimate vocation. God ultimately calls all to a spousal relationship with Him. Since he chose to reveal Himself to us as masculine, this means that in relation to him, every human soul is a bride. John Paul II says to consecrated women, "You help the church and all mankind to experience a 'spousal' relationship to God, one which magnificently expresses the fellowship which God wishes to establish with his creatures."[17]

Special challenges that women face

All persons wanting to live a virtuous life in a fallen world will face innumerable challenges, many of which are common to men and to women. But a number of the difficulties we encounter will be a direct result of our vocation as men and as women, respectively – and so they will be different in each case. While there are countless difficulties we could consider, we will look at a few that seem most universal and most common, though every reader will probably not be able to relate to some, and wish that others were included. I will first spend some time on difficulties related to motherhood, and then turn to more general challenges that women face.

Difficulties surrounding the vocation of biological motherhood

a. Modern society's downplaying of motherhood

One of the most serious attacks of secular society on the family, is the attack, not just on motherhood itself, but on the *image* of motherhood. Even for the woman who knows that there can be no greater natural vocation than motherhood, it can be a great effort for her to resist within herself a negative sense that as a mother, she is "just a housewife". Modernity would have us believe that one becomes a mother only if one has no talents, no interests, no gifts – in this case one "defaults" into tending a family full time.

But our reflections on the gifts of the woman lead us to see the great importance of motherhood. There is no more important task in earthly existence than to love the child, to lay the foundation for his life – both earthly and eternal – in its most important aspects.[18] The mother has in her care the most precious and most fragile of creatures – the child – and the family as a center of love. Once we understand how important motherhood is, and how important love is, we no longer wonder that the enemies of God would attack motherhood. This is one of the most efficient ways they have of causing deep suffering for the person in his earthly existence, and threatening his salvation – by weakening the foundations of his spiritual, emotional, and psychological life.

b. What of the woman without a natural disposition to love?

When we say that women are "by nature" disposed to love in this way, this does not mean that every individual woman has the same capacity for love. There are many factors that effect a person's capacity to love – everything from the "talent" they have from God, to their formation within the family of origin, to the influence of the wider society, to their individual free choices. This brings us to an important question. What about the woman who finds herself without a deep natural capacity for the vocation to which she is called?

No matter how much or little a particular woman is naturally disposed to love, we can still speak of a vocation of motherhood which is universal. In being "mother", the woman plays a role which only she can play; and this role requires certain things of her. If she keeps this always in mind, she will at every moment commit herself with her freedom to giving what only a mother can give. And this free commitment *is* love! Even if it doesn't flow spontaneously from a "full" heart, this commitment to love will make all the difference for the atmosphere within the family. The woman who simply "gives up" because she is not good at loving is completely different from the woman who commits herself to loving, despite her deficiencies. This woman will also over time grow in her ability to love.

c. All love must be freely given, because the tasks of motherhood are not easy

This leads us to see that all love must be freely given; it must come from a solid commitment of the will. Freedom is like the root of a tree, that is the hearty and dependable source of what grows on that tree. Even the woman who is "very feminine" by nature, should not simply love "automatically", as if her nature "makes her do it". Love is a gift, coming from one person to another, and so must be freely given.

This is also important, because even the most naturally disposed to love will at times find their hearts dry, or empty, or unable to give because of their own neediness. And even more: it is well known to every mother that in its day-to-day demands motherhood can be difficult in the greatest degree. The woman may long for the life of motherhood; she may long to give love to a child, and to receive the love of a child; but none of this means that she longs for the hardships that come with motherhood.

The greatest love will be tested by the burdens of the daily life of the mother, and the woman will wonder how she is supposed to love in the midst of them; she may, in fact, find that she is not able to. But in these moments, there is still much left for the woman to do: the commitment of her will to her child, to her family, will radiate through her way of being – and will in some way provide for the love that she cannot give at that moment. As we said above: this *will* be her way of loving in these moments.

d. Does mothering conflict with other gifts of the woman?
What of the mother who has some talents which might seem to stand in competition with mothering? Our thoughts on this point will be important for the woman who has natural gifts besides mother-love, or maybe even

some gift in greater abundance than the gift of loving. Should this woman give herself to her family, or should she pursue the development of her other "talents", or some service which she is capable of giving? If the woman discerns that she is called to become mother, and responds to this call, then she can be sure of her first calling: *to live motherhood*. As we saw, the child has a right to her love, and so long as she has brought a child into the world, she has an obligation to commit herself to that love.

Would God give an ability to the woman that seems to be a real part of who she is – and then not allow her to use it? This cannot be. The woman can be sure, that in giving herself to her family, she will be able to use and develop these gifts. In the beginning, this is not easy to see; the young mother will at first feel as though many of her special talents have to be put aside for the sake of her family. But in time she will see that this is not so. The openness of heart she turns towards her children will be the openness through which God places in her ideas for new and creative ways of exercising her gifts.

There may of course be some special cases where a woman finds herself in the situation of not being able to exercise her talents and pursue her interests, at least for a time. This woman is surely being asked to make a sacrifice. But it is a sacrifice made in the service of love, and so she should never be afraid that such a sacrifice could limit her fulfillment and her happiness. If she makes this sacrifice freely, and asks often for the grace that comes with her state in life, she will soon discover the treasures of living for love.

For working mothers

Many women with families find themselves in the position of having to work outside the home for a wage. In these cases, it is important for the woman to nevertheless endeavor to make her home the "center of gravity" of her life and being. While the working mother should embrace her situation fully and joyfully, with confidence in God's providence, it is nevertheless important for her to acknowledge within herself that the situation is less than ideal for her children. This inner acknowledgement will help to order and prioritise the activities in her life, so that her instinct in the face of choices will be to create as much space for mothering as she is able to in her particular situation. Children are capable of feeling keenly this attitude of the mother, and even without her verbal communication of it they will accept her being away from the home in a different way.

The mother should daily remind herself of the importance of her presence and love in the life of the family, so that when she is home she is aware of the child's need for her. After a full day's work outside the home the woman will inevitably be tired; but what she needs to give the child isn't so much a matter of energy as much as a matter of where she centers her being. What the child needs is to be "embraced" and held by the mother's look of attentive love, a look that sees the child as an individual, with his own inner life, with his own feelings and experiences, with the need to be "seen" – and this "embrace" is primarily a way of being on the part of the mother.

Nevertheless, the communication of this affirming love will require that some amount of time be devoted exclusively to the members of the family. Upon the woman's return home, the practical side of life will always threaten to sweep away the personal dimension. But before entering into the chores, every effort should be made by the mother to set aside some minutes for being physically and emotionally directly present to the children: engaging them in conversation, holding them physically, or sharing some activity together. Once the household tasks begin, persons should still remain the focus, and the tasks entered into not for their own sake, but as the matter of love and relationship. (Children are "geniuses" at picking up on this and running with it!) The fact that the woman will accomplish these things better on some days than on others, depending on how taxing her day has been, should not cause her distress; her commitment and her efforts will by themselves make all the difference for family life.

While it is a great boon for the family if, in the event of the mother's having to work, the father is able to remain at home with the child, even so the father's presence cannot supply for her absence. When she returns home after work, she should be ready to give to her child what only she can give.

More general challenges that women face

a. To love well, the woman must have a relationship with Christ

We have seen that the woman's calling includes being available for persons in a unique way, providing a "home" where the person can dwell secure. But this vocation to love others means that the woman herself has a great desire for love, for intimacy, for another heart to be home for her. Only God, in the person of Jesus, can meet the woman in her profound desire for love.

It is through a sincere and faithful spiritual life that the woman will draw close to the Heart of God, who is at every moment offering the infinitely deep, tender, personal love for which she longs. He waits for her, at every moment inviting her to drink more and more deeply from love's spring in Him. Prayer therefore must be the bedrock of her life. Her state in life will determine whether she is able to spend more or less time in prayer, and whether that prayer can always be deeply meditative or must sometimes (or even often) be simply a faithful repetition of some routine. But long or short, an authentic contact with the Lord who is never absent is always possible, and is vital for keeping her filled as she pours herself out for others. When possible, the woman should frequently receive the Sacraments, especially the Eucharist, "the sacrament of love". In spiritual reading, she will find a support and a defense against her own insecurity, worldly pressures, passing fads, and other influences that would threaten her ability to love well

Her relationship with Christ will then be the cornerstone for her human love-relationships, both deepening them, and purifying them. If her love for others is an overflow of the intimate love between her and Christ, this will guarantee that her love is truly selfless, and not self-seeking. If she is anchored in God's unconditional love, revealed in Christ on the cross, she will have the courage to remain vulnerable in the face of the difficulties surrounding earthly love, instead of becoming closed and resentful. If she knows herself to be forgiven by God in His love, she will be able to forgive those who offend against her love.

b. Desire for love and communion could also create the danger of settling for counterfeits

The readiness of the woman to be available for others carries with it the danger of allowing others to use her. For her to avoid this, she must have an inner sense of her own worth – she must know that she has been "willed by the Creator for her own sake", and may not be used by another. But if the woman's heart is not centered in God, there will always be a danger that her great thirst for love will mislead her into counterfeits – into false and superficial substitutes for love.

Once again – the woman must have a genuine spiritual life. As she reflects, for example, on the Gospel accounts of Christ's dealings with women, she will discover a God who respects the equal dignity of women with men, who shows reverence for their freedom, who never does violence to their heart. She will find a God who always exercises an infinite sensitivity in all of His dealings with them, who shows them the most tender forgiveness, and who calls them to the full dignity of the Sons of God through repentance. By contemplating God's reverence for her, by experiencing her own responsibility in the light of His calling her by name, she will become ever more filled with a living knowledge of her own worth.

This inner sense of her own dignity will then naturally translate into how she carries herself in her external behavior. By her manner, by the way she speaks and moves, others will be called upon to respect her personal dignity. How she presents herself to others should be a "call" and if necessary, a challenge to them to reverence her, and not to attempt use her as a means for their own pleasure and purposes.

c. Modesty in dress

Modesty in clothing for women has always been part of the Christian tradition. For a woman in contemporary culture, living the spirit of Christian modesty is particularly challenging. The woman wants to keep up with fashion, but this is becoming increasingly difficult. It is very important that, in her striving to go against the cultural current, the woman understand why modesty is so important.

Contrary to what its detractors would say, the Christian tradition of modesty in dress did not come about because of a fear of the body, or because of a fear of sexuality. Christianity has a completely different reason for covering certain parts of the body – for through the Incarnation, and the revelation of God's plan for its redemption, the dignity and beauty of the body came to light with new clarity. Why, then, this tradition of modesty?

Man and woman are unique among intelligent beings: unlike God and the angels, they are made up of body and soul – of matter and spirit. These two come together to form *one single being*. The body is not like an outer shell, completely removed form the body. Instead, the body *expresses* and *reveals* the soul; in some way, we can say that the body has the soul present in itself. Think of how a smile, or a hug, or a frown, are not just physical postures, but convey the spiritual realities of happiness, affection, and anger. What one does with the body, then, is not disconnected from the soul. Think of how it hurts our heart when someone slaps us in the face; and think of how the our heart is filled with warmth when someone gives us a sincere smile.

Modesty is based on this truth, of the connection between the body and the soul in the human person. There are parts of the body that are meant to convey *love*, and make possible a gift of self in love which is *total*, *permanent*, *exclusive*, and of the *deepest intimacy*. Because of their unique connection with love and total self-gift, these parts of the body call for a kind of special veiling. These parts of the body, since they are linked to the intimate "secret" of sexuality, should not be flaunted, any more than we would want to tell just anyone the intimate thoughts of our heart.

With the elevation of marriage to a Sacrament, the body is taken up into the life of the spirit in another way: the body becomes a sacrament of the grace of Christ. And so the Christian has yet another reason to preserve the dignity of the sexual sphere by modest clothing.

d. Self-mastery and self-discipline purify the woman's gifts
Finally, if the woman is truly to stand in service to others, there is a need for self-mastery and self-discipline in her life. One of the many mantras of today's culture is, "Let yourself go!" Indulge your desires, indulge your

cravings, indulge your whims – because, as we're often reminded, "You deserve it!" But a woman who lives in this way becomes controlled by these desires – and eventually comes to belong to *them*, and not to *herself*. How can she then "give herself away" in the self-gift of love, if she doesn't belong to herself to begin with? The many gifts of the woman can become her enemies, imprisoning her – everything from her physical beauty, to her rich emotional life, to her ability and desire to relate to other persons.

To give herself to others, the woman must first possess herself – and this she attains through *self-discipline and sacrifice*. She must always ask herself: What does the present moment require of me? Not: What do I feel like doing, or having? And often to do the right thing, she will have to die to herself. By means of these many small deaths, she frees herself of the captivity of her own tendencies, subjective desires, and drives, and becomes truly sovereign over her own being. So that when she chooses to give herself to another, in any form of service or self-gift, she is ready to do so – and is not enslaved by her own self-centeredness.

Conclusion

As we aim for becoming genuine women, through the gift of self to others, let us look to Mary, the virgin-mother, and most perfect of all women:

The church sees in Mary the highest expression of the 'feminine genius,' and she finds in her a source of constant inspiration. Mary called herself the 'handmaid of the Lord' (Lk 1:38). Through obedience to the word of God she accepted her lofty yet not easy vocation as wife and mother in the family of Nazareth. Putting herself at God's service, she also put herself at the service of others: a service of love.[19]

The woman becomes perfect when she becomes the "handmaid of the Lord", ready to serve Him and those to whom He calls her. I would like to end with the words of John Paul II, the pope who had such sensitivity for women – for their dignity, for their special sufferings, for their unique calling:

Therefore the Church gives thanks for each and every woman: for mothers, for sisters, for wives; for women consecrated to God in virginity; for women dedicated to the many human beings who await the gratuitous love of another person; for women who watch over the human persons in the family, which is the fundamental sign of the human community; for women who work professionally, and who at times are burdened by a great social responsibility; for "perfect" women and for "weak" women – for all women as they have come forth from the heart of God in all the beauty and richness of their femininity; as they have been embraced by his eternal love; as, together with men, they are pilgrims on this earth, which is the temporal "homeland" of all people and is transformed sometimes into a "valley of tears"; as they assume, together with men, a common responsibility for the destiny of humanity according to daily necessities and according to that definitive destiny which the human family has in God himself, in the bosom of the ineffable Trinity.[20]

Endnotes

[1] Second Vatican Council Closing Speech, December 8, 1965.

[2] *Gaudium et spes* §24. This is one of the central documents of the Second Vatican Council, called in English "the Pastoral Constitution on the Church in the Modern World". The Latin title is translated as "The joys and hopes", which are simply the first words of the document. The first sentence of the document reads: "The joys and the hopes, the griefs and the anxieties of the men of this age, especially those who are poor or in any way afflicted, these are the joys and hopes, the griefs and anxieties of the followers of Christ."

[3] *Gaudium et spes* §24. This sentence is perhaps the one most often quoted by Pope John Paul II in his writings.

[4] *Mulieris dignitatem* §2.

[5] *Mulieris dignitatem* §29.

[6] *Mulieris dignitatem* §18.

[7] "Affectivity" is another word for the emotions. It comes from the idea that when we feel emotions is it because we have been "affected" by something.

[8] This is what John Paul II seems to mean when he says that, "Perhaps more than men, women acknowledge the person, because they see persons with their hearts."[8]

[9] *Mulieris dignitatem* §30.

[10] Theodore Ratisbonne, *The Life and Times of St. Bernard* (Trans. H.E. Mannin. New York: P.J. Kenedy & Sons, 1902), 1.

[11] Edith Stein writes of the decisive role that woman can play in society, if only they retain their uniquely feminine way of being: "Thus the participation of women in the most diverse professional disciplines could be a blessing for the entire society, private or public, precisely if the specifically feminine ethos would be preserved." "The Ethos of Woman's Professions", in *Essays on Woman* (trans. Freda Mary Oben, 2nd ed. Washington, D.C.: ICS Publications, 1996), 50.

[12] *Mulieris dignitatem* §30.

[13] *Salvifici dolores*, §29.

[14] We find in *Mulieris dignitatem*, §20: "One cannot correctly understand virginity—a woman's consecration in virginity—without referring to spousal love. It is through this kind of love that a person becomes a gift for the other."

[15] John Paul II writes in this regard: "The naturally spousal predisposition of the feminine personality finds a response in virginity understood in this way. Women, called from the very 'beginning' to be loved and to love, in a vocation to virginity find Christ first of all as the Redeemer who 'loved until the end' through his total gift of self; and they respond to this gift with a 'sincere gift' of their whole lives." *Mulieris dignitatem*, §20.

[16] *Mulieris dignitatem* §21.

[17] *Letter to Women* §2.

[18] In his *Letter to Women* John Paul II thanks women who are mothers, saying that through motherhood "[they] become God's own smile upon the newborn child".

19 *Letter to women* §10.

20 *Mulieris dignitatem* §30.